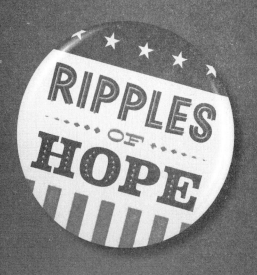

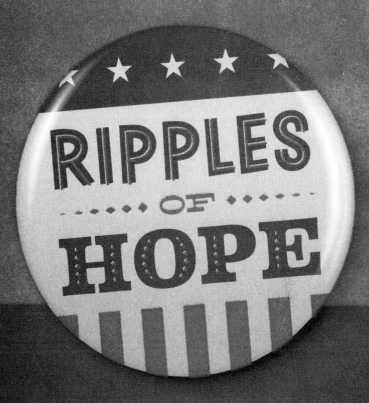

RIPPLES OF HOPE

YOUR GUIDE TO
☞ ELECTING ☜
A NEW PRESIDENT

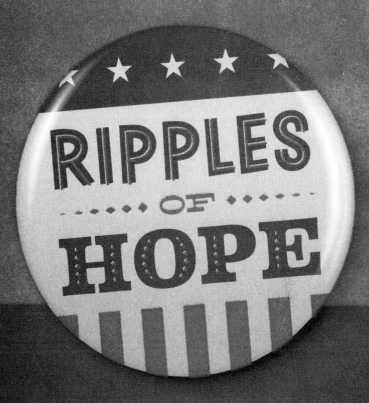

★ DAVID PLOUFFE ★
Campaign Manager *for* PRESIDENT BARACK OBAMA

HENRY HOLT AND COMPANY
New York

HENRY HOLT AND COMPANY, *Publishers since 1866*
Henry Holt® is a registered trademark of
Macmillan Publishing Group, LLC
120 Broadway, New York, New York 10271 • mackids.com

ISBN 978-1-250-25975-2
Library of Congress Control Number 2019955644

Our books may be purchased in bulk for promotional, educational,
or business use. Please contact your local bookseller or the Macmillan
Corporate and Premium Sales Department at (800) 221-7945 ext. 5442
or by email at MacmillanSpecialMarkets@macmillan.com.

First edition, 2020 / *Designed by* RAPHAEL GERONI

Printed in the United States of America by LSC Communications,
Harrisonburg, Virginia

1 3 5 7 9 10 8 6 4 2

For EVERETT and VIVIAN—

I can't wait to live in a world you help shape

CONTENTS

Introduction

You probably aren't old enough to vote yet, and because of that, you may think there isn't much you can do to help decide who our next president should be. But I want you to know that you *can* have something to do with it. You can make a huge difference. Maybe *the* difference. And I hope you will.

The next presidential election might be even more important to you than it is to the adults you know. There is a lot at stake.

Some of your hopes and fears probably match those of my own kids.

"Can't we stop all the killing in schools?"

"Will Earth even be livable for my children?"

"Why is there still so much hate and racism?"

"I don't want tens of thousands of dollars in school loans like my older brother has."

"We'll fix it all if we get the chance."

"Why do we still fight wars?"

"Most people are good. I wish more of our leaders were like them."

The winner of the next presidential election will need to make a lot of decisions that will affect your future. It must be frustrating that you can't vote on who that person will be. But while you can't yet cast a ballot, you *can* cast your influence far and wide on those who will be voting.

You don't have a VOTE, but you have a VOICE.

And if you use it often enough, and with enough persistence, you can make the difference in this election.

My hope for this book is to share with younger readers just why I believe your voices are so important and to provide specifics about the most effective ways you can raise them up during this election, and beyond. I should also make clear here at the start that this is not a nonpartisan book. I have a strong point of view. I managed President Barack Obama's campaign. I am a Democrat, and I want the Democratic nominee to win the presidential election in 2020.

The 2020 presidential election will be close. Donald Trump will probably get at least 45 percent of the vote, maybe more. And a bunch of kids your age will be supporting him too and finding ways to help him win reelection.

Everyone has the right to hold their own views and to support the candidate of their choice. We live in a politically divided country. Maybe most of the people where you live think Donald Trump is doing a great job. It's probably more likely, since you are reading this book, that many of the people you know think Donald Trump is doing a terrible job. But if you believe for a moment that Trump is guaranteed to lose because a lot of the people you know don't like him, that can be dangerous.

If you care about this next election and if, like me, you hope the Democratic nominee will win, the most important thing to do is understand that Trump could win again.

Once you accept that, it's time to focus on what you can do to ensure the Trump administration only gets four years, not eight.

Four years is, frankly, enough. This president is making the climate crisis worse, making it harder for families to have health care and afford school, discriminating against the LGBTQ community, and alienating our longtime allies. If he has eight years in office, he will do double the damage.

You have the power to make sure this doesn't happen to our country and our world.

When I managed President Barack Obama's campaign, we won in large part because of the support and passion of young people in America. Yes, some were eighteen-to-twenty-five-year-olds who voted in big numbers for Obama. They also worked heroically on the campaign. But an underappreciated part of why we won was the support of people under eighteen. Kids your age who supported Obama so strongly that they talked to their families about what it would mean if he won. Kids who asked to volunteer on the campaign and dragged other friends and family with them. Kids who created posters and poems and songs, which motivated others to get involved.

I think NOTHING is more powerful than a young person believing deeply in something.

If you have that strong belief, if you do not want to live in a country that has Donald Trump as its president, you can be the secret weapon that makes sure his time in office comes to an end.

I have a fifteen-year-old son and an eleven-year-old daughter. They were heartbroken on election night in 2016, especially because I made the mistake of being so confident Hillary Clinton would win. They have the passion to elect a new president, and more creativity, thirst for social justice, and energy than I've ever had. I know there are millions across the country like them. If you are one of those millions, this book will offer you some ideas about how to channel that passion, talent, and belief in ways that can make a difference in the presidential campaign.

If this election is about anything, it's about your future. Don't let that future be dictated to you by others—seize the moment and shape the future you want for yourself and your friends.

Senator Robert F. Kennedy, two years before he was assassinated in 1968, gave an important speech opposing apartheid in South Africa.

He famously said,

"It is from numberless diverse acts of courage and belief that human history is shaped. Each time a [person] stands up for an ideal, or acts to improve the lot of others, or strikes out against injustice, he sends forth a tiny ripple of hope, and crossing each other from a million different centers of energy and daring, those ripples build a current which can sweep down the mightiest walls of oppression and resistance."

You can be that RIPPLE OF HOPE.

◆◆◆◆◆◆

YOU

can do this.

◆◆◆◆◆◆

1

YOUNG ACTIVISTS ARE CHANGING THE WORLD

LOOK ALL AROUND YOU FOR THE EVIDENCE.

MARCH FOR OUR LIVES

After a gunman's brutal rampage left seventeen dead and seventeen wounded at Marjory Stoneman Douglas High School in Parkland, Florida, a group of student survivors started the March for Our Lives movement. They have played an enormous role in mobilizing people all over the country, young and old, to become activists to reduce gun violence. While our national leaders in Washington have been unable or unwilling to do anything to make it safer for you to go to school, the kids from Parkland—Emma González, David Hogg, Jaclyn Corin, Cameron Kasky, and Alex Wind, among others—have helped change local laws all over the country and helped elect new leaders who will put stopping gun violence at the top of their list. And most of these student activists couldn't yet vote when they made that happen.

GRETA THUNBERG

Greta Thunberg, a young environmental activist from Sweden, has raised global awareness of climate change and has rallied students worldwide to become more active in efforts to fight it, inspiring millions of adults around the planet to become more engaged too. She is well-known for telling it like it is. She spoke to members of a Senate task force when she visited America, and when they expressed admiration for her and other youth activists, she said, "Please save us your praise. We don't want it. Don't invite us here to tell us how inspiring we are without doing anything about it."

She spoke forcefully at the most recent meeting of the United Nations General Assembly, telling leaders from around the world:

"You are failing us, but young people are starting to understand your betrayal. The eyes of all future generations are upon you, and if you choose to fail us, I say we will never forgive you."

WOW.

For this, political conservatives and climate change deniers mocked her for her looks and clothes and even questioned her intelligence and mental health.

Yet she persisted, and still does.

LITTLE MISS FLINT

Mari Copeny, also known as Little Miss Flint, brought awareness to the water crisis in Flint, Michigan, when she wrote a letter to President Obama at age eight. And she continues to advocate for her community today at age twelve.

She says,

"My generation will fix this mess of a government. Watch us."

NADIA NAZAR

Nadia Nazar is a seventeen-year-old activist and artist from Baltimore, Maryland. At age fifteen, she cofounded the youth-led climate organization Zero Hour with three friends she met online. As an artist, Nadia uses her creativity to support her activism. She says, "[Art is] an easy way to get a message across, because people don't like to listen to what others are saying. But if you look at a visual piece, hear music, or experience a piece of artwork, they contain symbols and messages that are universal to most people."

RAMON CONTRERAS

amon Contreras, now twenty years old, founded Youth Over Guns, an organization dedicated to raising awareness about gun violence in black and brown communities, after he lost a friend to gun violence in high school. He organized a ten-thousand-person march across the Brooklyn Bridge, during which student activists carried a casket to symbolize deaths from violence in communities of color. He is currently working as a strategist to inspire and encourage more people of color to enter the political arena.

XIUHTEZCATL MARTINEZ

Xiuhtezcatl Martinez is a nineteen-year-old indigenous climate activist and hip-hop artist. As Youth Director of Earth Guardians, he helped ban the use of pesticides in city parks in his hometown of Boulder, Colorado.

He has been a passionate activist since he was SIX years old.

AND YOU!

These are just a few examples of young activists who are raising their voices and insisting on being heard. There are many, many more. Kids like these—kids like you—can and will change the world. All young people have the right to participate and engage with their elected officials. It is your future that is being decided by the people in power. If you haven't had a chance yet to get involved, or if you have and you're ready for more, the upcoming presidential election is your golden opportunity. November 3, 2020, might be the most important Election Day in American history. We need your passion, your creativity, and your energy to help elect a new president. We need you. Maybe that seems like a lot of responsibility.

But when *you* becomes *we*, and *we* becomes *us*—millions and millions of young people coming together—that becomes a force too POWERFUL to be DENIED.

2

HOW A PRESIDENTIAL ELECTION WORKS

FIRST YOU NEED YOUR NOMINEES

Before we can get to the presidential election, we need to determine who the nominees will be. We have a mostly two-party system here in the United States. While there are other political parties, the two majority parties, Democratic and Republican, dominate our political process. So the Democrats need to decide who their candidate will be, and the Republicans need to decide who theirs will be.

Presidential elections take place every four years. The Twenty-Second Amendment to the Constitution of the United States says that a person can only be elected to serve as president two times, for a total of eight years. If the current president is eligible for reelection, then that person will almost always be their party's nominee. For the 2020 election, although there may be one or two long-shot Republican candidates willing to challenge him, we can be sure the Republican nominee will be Donald Trump.* The Republican Party announces its formal nominations for president and vice president at the Republican National Convention.

*A Note on Impeachment

You will have heard people talking about impeachment in regard to Donald Trump. So what is impeachment, anyway?

The roots of the word impeachment mean "to prevent" or "to catch." (It doesn't have anything to do with peaches.) And if a president is impeached, which is an action taken by the House of Representatives, it doesn't mean that they are automatically removed from office. Impeachment is a process through which a government official, in this case a president, may be charged with one or more crimes committed while in office. And eventually, if the United States Senate convicts the president, they can be removed from office. In United States history, impeachment of the president is very rare. It has happened (or come close to happening) only three times before. And so far, a United States president has never been removed from office by the process of impeachment.

If you are reading this and Donald Trump is still our president, he may have been impeached but he has not been convicted and removed from office. The only way for him to be removed is if he loses the election.

THE DEMOCRATIC NOMINEE

There are a lot of candidates vying for the 2020 Democratic presidential nomination. Maybe you already know some of them or have a favorite you hope will be the nominee. This field of candidates will get narrowed down in a series of primary elections and caucuses, where the voters in each state have a chance to vote for the Democratic candidate they think would make the best nominee. All of this culminates in the Democratic National Convention, where the Democrats will formally choose the party's nominees for president and vice president.

I'm simplifying this part of the process so I can get to the postnomination battle. I'm leaving out details about debates and delegates, and the difference between a caucus and a primary. All of that is important, and I encourage you to find out more if you are interested, but my hope for this book is that it will help you support the Democratic nominee, whoever that may be! So, onward.

ELECTING A PRESIDENT

In a direct popular vote, like you may have in school, whoever gets the most votes wins the election for student council or class president.

That's also the case for congressional elections in the United States. In 2018, for example, the Democrats won back majority control of the U.S. House of Representatives because more of their candidates won more votes than the Republican candidates in their elections.

In those cases elections are simple. You get the most votes, you win. It's especially simple in a primarily two-party system as we have in

America. Other countries have a lot of political parties, so it's harder for one candidate or party to win a majority. Here, it's almost always a matter of whether the Democrat or Republican gets the most votes.

But the election for the presidency is not as simple. Perhaps you remember election night, 2016. You probably remember that Donald Trump won in a huge upset, which is what it's called when an election has a result very different from what many people expected. You probably remember that Trump won the election despite getting fewer votes than his opponent, Hillary Clinton. A lot fewer. He received three million fewer votes. Three million. That's more votes than the total number of votes cast in each of thirty-seven states in 2016.

How could that happen, and WHY is it so?

THE ELECTORAL COLLEGE

We can thank the founders of our country for many things, and we can blame them for the Electoral College, which makes it possible for a candidate to win the national popular vote and still lose the presidential election. The system the founders gave us led us to our current process: Rather than a direct election of all voters in all states—a national popular vote where whoever gets the most votes wins—presidential elections are decided state by state. Most states require the winner of their state's presidential vote be granted all the electoral votes of that state. Those electoral votes match the state's representation in Congress. Basically, you take the number of a state's representatives in the House (which is based on the population in the last census), add two for the senators (each state gets two), and you get the number of electoral votes. One exception is the District of Columbia, which gets three electoral votes even though it is not a state and does not have representation in Congress.

States with fewer people have fewer electoral votes; states with more people have more. Put all those states and their electoral votes together, and you have the system we still elect our presidents by today, the Electoral College.

In 2020, the most populous state in our union, California, will offer fifty-five electoral votes to the winner (fifty-three representatives and two senators), and seven states with the smallest populations will offer just three electoral votes to their winners. Alaska, Delaware, Montana, North Dakota, South Dakota, Vermont, and Wyoming all have only one representative and two senators in Congress.

538 AND 270—WHY DO THESE NUMBERS MATTER?

After Hawaii and Alaska were admitted as the forty-ninth and fiftieth states in the union, and after the Twenty-Third Amendment granted electoral votes to Washington, D.C., in 1961, the Electoral College was set at 538.

Every ten years, based on each state's population as counted by the census, the electoral votes are adjusted—states that have gained a lot of population may gain one or two, and those that have lost population may lose one or two.

But the number remains 538. You have to win a majority of the Electoral College votes to win the presidency.

Which means the magic number to get to the White House is 270. That's how many electoral votes you NEED to WIN.

Whether or not to abolish the Electoral College is frequently debated in this country. I hope our presidential election is changed so that all votes count equally no matter where you live and that the person who gets the most votes wins. It probably won't happen in my lifetime, but I hope it will in yours. But for now, everything you can and must do to help in this election can be boiled down to this simple mission:

270

It's the most important number for your future, and the planet's.

ELECTORAL COLLEGE MAP

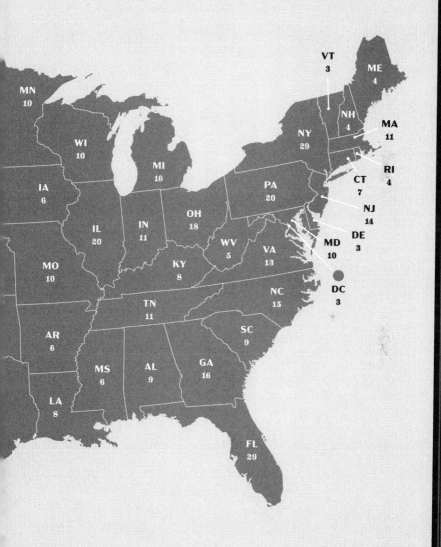

MN
10

ME
4

VT
3

WI
10

NH
4

NY
29

MA
11

IA
6

MI
16

RI
4

CT
7

IL
20

IN
11

OH
18

PA
20

NJ
14

MO
10

KY
8

WV
5

VA
13

DE
3

MD
10

AR
6

TN
11

NC
15

DC
3

MS
6

AL
9

SC
9

LA
8

GA
16

FL
29

3

BATTLEGROUND
STATES

OKAY, SO EVERY STATE HAS A NUMBER OF electoral votes, and together all fifty states plus Washington, D.C., add up to 538. And you need to win 270 of them to become president. So does that mean that if you are running a presidential campaign, you need to campaign in all fifty states to have the best chance of winning enough to be victorious?

Actually, no. Not by a long shot. In fact, only six to eight of our fifty states will be truly competitive in 2020—meaning they will be close enough that either candidate could win.

How could that be?

Well, many states have decided political leanings. In some, the Democratic candidate wins easily, and in others the Republican candidate wins without breaking a sweat.

In 2020, we can take it to the bank that the Democratic nominee will win California's fifty-five electoral votes, New York's twenty-nine, and New Jersey's fourteen. The Republican is a lock to win Arkansas's six, Tennessee's eleven, Kansas's six, and many of the southern and Great Plains states.

The states that are considered solidly Democratic or solidly Republican fluctuate over time due to shifts in demographics and political ideologies. Back in 1976, Democrat Jimmy Carter won the entire South apart from Virginia, and Republican Gerald Ford won almost all the New England states that are solidly Democratic now, as well as California and Illinois, which are also solidly blue today.

BLUE? WHAT DOES COLOR HAVE TO DO WITH IT?

Back in the 1970s, when color televisions began to overtake black-and-white sets in American homes, network news teams started coloring in states on maps of the United States as results came in on election night. Blue meant one candidate had won the state, red meant the other. The networks differed on who was blue and who was red at first. Some chose red for the Democrats and blue for the

Republicans or vice versa. But by 1996 they had settled on one color scheme: red for Republicans and blue for Democrats. In terms of political coverage, many states are now referred to by their current likely color—California is a blue state and Alabama is a red state.

For most of the country, over forty states, we are near certain what color will be filled in on election night.

PURPLE STATES

The battle will be for the states where the outcome is uncertain and likely to be close. The results in these states will determine who wins the presidency.

These are commonly called battleground states because that is where the political war will be waged. These are the places where almost all the money raised by the campaign will be spent. Many more campaign workers will be placed in these states, and the candidates will spend almost all their time campaigning there rather than in the rest of the country.

People like me, who are or have been responsible for winning presidential races, live, breathe, and sleep battleground states. They are all that matter. They have become known as purple states—neither red nor blue, they could go either way.

How do we know which states are likely to be battlegrounds? A lot of research factors into it, but mainly it's studying recent elections to look at trends and results; conducting polls to find out how voters in that state say they are going to vote; examining the condition of the economy in the state, which is usually a critical factor in how voters make their decisions; and considering what unique strengths or weaknesses each of the candidates brings to particular states or regions. Perhaps a candidate comes from that area, for example, or has special appeal to certain types of voters such as young people or minorities or blue-collar workers.

WISCONSIN, MICHIGAN, AND PENNSYLVANIA

In 2020, we can count on a few states being certain battlegrounds. Until 2016, no Republican candidate had won all three of the states of Wisconsin, Michigan, and Pennsylvania since Ronald Reagan back in 1984. No Democrat had lost any of them since 1988.

Donald Trump won all three, and that is the major reason he won the presidency. He will likely need to win them all again, or at least two of the three, to be reelected. And the Democratic candidate will have an exceedingly tough time winning the presidency without those states in their column. Much of the political battle will be fought there.

FLORIDA

Florida is also likely to be a huge
battleground. Although much is changing
in terms of states' political preferences and
behavior, the one thing we've been able to count
on in recent presidential elections is Florida
being painfully close.

Donald Trump won Florida narrowly in
2016; Barack Obama did too in 2008 and 2012.
George W. Bush won it by a wider margin in
2004, but most famously in 2000 he won it by
a mere 537 votes out of over five million votes
cast, making it the state that delivered him the
presidency. Even back in the 1990s Florida was
competitive, with Bill Clinton losing it in 1992
and winning it in 1996.

The Sunshine State had statewide elections
with razor-thin margins for governor and U.S.
senator in 2018. And in the next election,
Florida will be close again—and fiercely
contested. With twenty-nine electoral votes,

Florida is by far the largest battleground state, but the winner of Florida greatly enhances their odds of winning the presidency.

ARIZONA AND NORTH CAROLINA

The Democratic campaign will look to some red states from 2016 that could be winnable in 2020. Arizona, which saw a Democratic candidate win a U.S. Senate race in 2018, has been trending more Democratic. Larger numbers of Latino voters, who lean strongly Democratic, are voting at higher rates in Arizona. Suburban women voters in the state are also voting more reliably Democratic. Arizona could be as close as Wisconsin and Florida in 2020. Arizona has eleven electoral votes, one more than Wisconsin.

The Democratic nominee will also look to

North Carolina, a state Barack Obama narrowly won once and narrowly lost once. Although Hillary Clinton lost the state in 2016, the state still elected a Democrat for governor in a very close race that year. North Carolina offers a significant fifteen electoral votes.

Those are the six locks to be core battleground states. But both sides will look for additional opportunities, in part so they don't have to win every state they target. By competing in more states, a campaign can lose some and still win the election.

TEXAS

One big question will be the state of Texas. Because of the growing political power of the Latino population and younger and suburban voters trending Democratic, Texas could be a core battleground in 2020.

Beto O'Rourke showed what's possible by almost winning it in a Senate race in 2018. Texas has thirty-eight electoral votes, which have been considered safely Republican for a long time. If that changes, it could alter the Electoral College chess match enormously.

GEORGIA

Like Texas, it's not a question of if, but rather when, Georgia will become a core battleground state that a Democratic nominee could win. Democrat Stacey Abrams ran a heroic governor's race in 2018 and lost by only 1.4 percentage points. Strong voter registration and Democratic turnout combined with a candidate who can dominate among younger and suburban voters could put the Peach State in play.

LESS LIKELY BATTLEGROUNDS

There are states that Barack Obama won twice that Donald Trump flipped red, like Iowa and Ohio, that the Democratic candidate will strongly consider targeting. But these states are further down the battleground list in terms of priority and winnability, if they even make the cut. Why? Because Trump showed enormous political strength in those states, and demographically, they are not adding young and minority voters at the same rate as other states. Obama won thirty-eight counties in Iowa in 2012; Hillary Clinton only won six in 2016. It will take a great Democratic candidate and probably a struggling economy to put Iowa and Ohio back in play in 2020.

This makes me sad because Ohio was the state, in both 2008 and 2012, that put Obama over the top, and Iowa was where Barack Obama burst onto the national scene by winning the Iowa caucuses in 2008. I see them both blue in my mind. I hope that doesn't become a fading memory.

The Trump campaign will hope to be competitive and put pressure on the Democratic campaign in a number of other states. Nevada, Minnesota, Maine, New Hampshire, New Mexico, and Virginia are all states that Obama and Clinton won and that more often than not produce Democratic wins in other statewide races. I believe the Democratic candidate has a better chance to win Arizona or North Carolina than Trump has to win any of these six states, but the Trump campaign's goal, even if he doesn't win the states, will be to force his opponent to spend money, time, and attention on them, diverting resources from some core battlegrounds.

Remember, a presidential campaign is not a national election. It is a series of select state campaigns.

Now that you know how a presidential election works and where the real action will take place, let's dive into what the Democratic presidential campaign will be doing to help our candidate win the battleground states and to help Democrats around the country win everywhere.

HOW A CAMPAIGN WORKS

VOLUNTEERS—WHY DO WE NEED THEM?

You may already spend time volunteering in your local community. Perhaps you stack and sort cans and produce at a local food bank, hold bake sales to raise money for your school, work at your local animal shelter, or help clean up a local park. And if you haven't had a chance to be a volunteer yet, you might have a parent or older sibling who gives time outside of work and family to help the community and those in need.

Almost all local charitable, or nonprofit, groups have employees whose full-time job is to work on the cause of their organization. The gap between what they need to do versus the number of workers they can employ is often large. It would cost far too much to hire all the full-time or even part-time workers to meet the demands of the organization. That gap gets filled by volunteers. These are people who help out, maybe for a few hours each week or month.

By giving the valuable resource of their time, they help support the causes and groups they believe in.

Volunteers are the ones who make it possible for many charitable organizations to accomplish their goals and serve those at the center of their mission. It's the same for a political campaign.

In a presidential campaign, or really any political campaign, it's the volunteers who make it all work. Volunteers can make the difference between winning and losing. And yes, kids can volunteer. You do not have to wait until you reach a certain age to volunteer to support a cause or a candidate you believe in. You just need the permission and support of your family.

THE GROUND GAME OF A CAMPAIGN

Let's take a step back and look at how a campaign is organized. By the time of the election, the nominees will have several thousand staff on board. These are full-time workers whose jobs are to work on the campaign. Most of them will be what we call field organizers. Many of them will be young adults in their early- to mid-twenties. The field organizers will be based in the battleground states, and each will be responsible for organizing a particular area in one of those states.

What exactly does organizing mean? In our normal lives it could mean organizing the clothes in our drawers, or the apps on our phones, or keeping school materials and assignments in folders so we know where to find them.

In politics, organizing has a slightly different meaning.

The field organizers in Tucson, Arizona, or Harrisburg, Pennsylvania, or Chippewa Falls, Wisconsin, will be responsible for creating and managing the entire operation that will be needed to win enough votes in their area for their candidate.

And this is where all of those volunteers come into play. The only paid employee of the campaign in an area is that one field organizer. But they need hundreds of people—volunteers—from that local area to do all the work it will take to hit their numeric goals and win.

A local field organizer will recruit volunteers to take on bigger roles and more responsibility as precinct captains or neighborhood team leaders. Precincts are how voters are grouped based on their home address. Each precinct is given a polling place where its voters go to vote on Election Day. Precincts average about eight hundred voters each, and election results are tabulated and reported at the precinct level.

A precinct captain reports directly to the field organizer. Depending on the size of the precinct, the captain may have neighborhood team leaders who oversee a portion of the precinct. Let's say we have our precinct captain, Everett, and he in turn has four neighborhood team leaders working with him. Most of these people will have day jobs, or school, along with family responsibilities. So on top of their other work, they are spending hours a day on the campaign. Everett and the team leaders and their families are making a big sacrifice.

They are heroes we can all be proud of in the effort to elect a new president.

BUT WHAT DO THEY DO?

First and most important, the field organizers, precinct captains, and neighborhood team leaders are trying to recruit other volunteers to help achieve their goals (more on those shortly). The campaign will have a list of people who signed up online to volunteer in that local area. They will also reach out to anyone in the area who has made a financial contribution to their candidate. Many great progressive groups like Swing Left and Indivisible encourage their members to sign up for volunteer activities. The local branch of the Democratic Party will have a list of people who have volunteered in previous elections, and our volunteer leaders will bring their own lists of people they think they can convince to join them.

Once the captains and leaders have recruited volunteers, they'll organize schedules for when people can help. Some volunteers will say they can give a set number of hours every week. Others may say they only have a little bit of time right before the election. The volunteer leaders keep track of all that information, so they know exactly who has time and when they have it. Then they can ask people for help when they are most likely able to say yes.

The next big job for the organizers is matching volunteers with opportunities by finding out what type of activity they are most interested in. There are a lot of different ways to help a presidential campaign locally. Perhaps the volunteer would enjoy being outside and walking through neighborhoods, knocking on the doors of voters. Perhaps they like calling people, either from their home with a list the campaign provides or from the local campaign office. Maybe they like working sign-in tables at events or want to drive people who need a ride to the polls. Maybe they like to write personal postcards encouraging people to register to vote or reminding them to go to the polls on Election Day.

All that information is collected, so people can be asked to participate in activities that match their interests.

VOTE GOALS

The ultimate job of the local precinct organization is simple, though the work is very hard: get the votes necessary to win. The campaign will set a goal for the number needed in each precinct.

Let's say we are talking about a precinct in Reading, Pennsylvania. The campaign thinks 365 votes are needed out of the precinct. They will have a number for every precinct in the state.

If you hit your vote goals in enough precincts, you usually win an election. If you don't, you lose.

So how do volunteers help get those 365 votes?

IT'S PRETTY
SIMPLE–

PEOPLE *talking* to *other* PEOPLE.

HOW DO WE KNOW WHO TO TALK TO?

Different categories of people and voters are critical in an election. These people will be the focus of local volunteer efforts.

First, there will be people who are not yet registered to vote. Based on a variety of factors such as age or neighborhood or information about their likes and habits, the campaign thinks some of these people would be likely to support their candidate if they did register and vote.

Second, there will be people who are registered but don't have a history of voting reliably. Voting history is publicly available for all registered voters in America. Not who they voted for—that's private—but whether or not they voted in previous elections. People may have registered to vote, but for whatever reason, when Election Day came, they never made it to the polls. Perhaps they were sick. Or didn't really follow the election closely. Or didn't like any of the candidates. In each precinct, the campaign will have a list of people who it thinks would almost certainly vote for the Democratic presidential candidate but may not vote at all.

Third, there will be a relatively small group of people who are undecided. They are most likely going to vote, but they are not sure which candidate they are going to vote for. These people are also commonly referred to as "swing" voters because most of this group does not vote reliably for one party or the other, as most voters in America do. They bounce around and vote for different parties and candidates depending on the year and election. Campaigns develop a sense of who these citizens are by conducting polls, using data analysis, and also from volunteers who talk to these conflicted voters and report them as truly undecided.

Campaign volunteers will be asked to engage in all sorts of activities like the ones mentioned previously—knocking on doors, making phone calls, working sign-in tables, writing postcards, and more—all aimed at getting these different groups of people in their area to register, turn out on Election Day, and ultimately vote for their candidate.

LEADING BY EXAMPLE

f you decide *you* want to get involved in the presidential campaign as a volunteer, you will not only be using your time and talents to make a difference, but you may also inspire other people to join you as well.

First, you should tell everyone you know who also wants to see a new president elected that you've decided to volunteer. Tell your friends and family why you want to do it and what you've learned, the types of volunteer activities you are interested in, and ask them to join you.

With close family members, you can do more than ask. You can insist. Tell your mom or uncle or older sibling who is always complaining about Trump that words of outrage are not enough.

They have to really get into the fight.

The fact that you are prepared to give your time to help shape your future will make a big impact. I won't say you should go so far as to make your family feel guilty, but I'd get pretty close.

Once you get your family on board, make a list of all the other people you might be able to convince to volunteer. Think about the issues or causes that you know they care about so you can make the best pitch about why they should get involved. Reach out to all of them and tell them you've decided to spend what time you can helping our nominee. Tell them why you've decided to help and why it can make a difference. Make sure they know that if the Democratic campaign doesn't have enough volunteers, Donald Trump will get reelected.

I would suggest talking to people in person or calling them rather than texting. If they hear your voice, people can get the fullest sense of your passion and commitment and you will also have a chance to answer questions they might have. Some people will be reluctant. You can ask them to please just give it a try. Tell them there is no commitment. They don't need to sign up for more than one volunteer shift. If it's not for them, they don't have to do it again.

Odds are they will; you just have to get them in the door.

Having more friends and family around will also make it more fun for you. You'll have more comfort and confidence heading into a campaign office for the first time with many people you know. You can share your thoughts and feelings about your volunteer activities with those close to you—what went well, what you liked, what was challenging, what gave you hope, and what made you concerned. It will be helpful to share and sort through these feelings.

You are also trying to change your country with those closest to you, and that can be one of the best feelings in the world.

As a volunteer, you are not a passive witness to this historic election. You are an important participant.

To experience that with close friends and family will be a strong bonding moment for all of you and an important memory that you can take forward in life.

There is a quote widely attributed to Dr. Martin Luther King Jr. that states, "In the end, we will remember not the words of our enemies, but the silence of our friends." None of us can afford to be silent in this election.

The stakes are too high, and the race will be too close.

Barack Obama often says, and believes to his core, that ordinary people joining together can do extraordinary things.

This election will be WON–or LOST–based on the actions, or inaction, of ordinary people.

The spirit of young people caring so deeply about the future of our country that they decide to devote their free time to hitting the streets and the phones to elect a new president is infectious. *You* can be the reason many others in your community decide to get more actively involved.

5

WHAT CAN KIDS DO?

So you've decided to volunteer to help our candidate. Yes! Now let's take a closer look at what you personally can do. You might not be old enough to be a field organizer or a precinct captain (yet), but there are many things you can do to help elect a new president.

I LIVE IN A BATTLEGROUND STATE!

f you live in a battleground state, then it is extra easy to participate directly in the presidential election. If you and your friends and family believe strongly that we need to defeat Donald Trump, and if you live at ground zero in the battle for the White House, you *must* come up with a plan and commit whatever time you can afford to volunteering to help make sure our candidate wins your home state.

Not to put too much pressure on you—never mind, I'll go ahead with the pressure.

If not you, who?

The Electoral College system is flawed, but it's the only one we have, and most people in the country do not live in battleground states. In reality, so many people in our country and the world are counting on those of you who do live in these critical states to do all you can to put an end to the Trump nightmare. Kids of Wisconsin, Michigan, Pennsylvania, Florida, Arizona, North Carolina, Texas, Georgia, Iowa, Ohio, Nevada, Minnesota, Maine, New Hampshire, New Mexico, and Virginia—you can do this!

Rather than be cowed by this responsibility, I hope you embrace it.

You have a front-row seat to history—history you will have a hand in making if you do all you can.

I DON'T LIVE IN A BATTLEGROUND STATE

For those of you who do not live in battleground states, being active in your own state is still important. Every effort matters, and there are ways to reach out to voters from wherever you are. But if your family is on board, and geography and finances make it possible for you as a group to travel to a battleground state for a day or a weekend, convince them to plan a trip to a place where your efforts can make the biggest difference.

For those of you who live within driving distance, this may be easier to accomplish. If you live in Wilmington, Delaware, which will go blue, plan family trips to help out in Pennsylvania. If you live in Mobile, Alabama, which will go red, plan to drive down to northern Florida to help the campaign there.

You and your family can sign up for volunteer shifts online. Let the local campaign offices in the battleground state know you will be visiting the area and want to help. The Democratic campaign and progressive organizations will also have buses available for people who want to travel across state lines, say from the Bay Area in California to Reno, Nevada, or from Chicago, Illinois, to Wisconsin and Michigan.

If you are passionate about this election and it is possible for your family, spend time on the ground where it will be decided. There is, of course, great and important work you can do closer to home, both for our nominee and for local Democratic candidates, but if you can, even if just for a couple of days, go where the heaviest action is. You'll never forget it.

The campaign offices in battleground states may also have lists of supporters willing to host out-of-town volunteers, to save people the cost of hotel rooms. You can ask your family to look into this if it might make a trip to a battleground state more affordable.

And if your family's circumstances make it possible for you to take regular family vacations, maybe just for one year, this year, think about trading in the trip to the beach or a theme park. If you all agree that this election is important enough, you could take that time and money and use it to help elect a new president.

VOTER REGISTRATION

In the United States, you need to be eighteen years old to vote. It used to be twenty-one, but it was changed to eighteen when the Twenty-Sixth Amendment to the Constitution was ratified in 1971. That was during the Vietnam War, and eighteen- and nineteen-year-olds were getting drafted into the military to fight. Many were coming home wounded, or not coming home at all.

Student organizers rightly asked, "If we are old enough to die for our country, surely we are old enough to vote?" Changing the Constitution is no small thing—another great example of young people leading the charge against steep odds.

You may think that's all it takes. You turn eighteen and you can vote. Sadly, no. Unlike many countries, like Sweden and Israel, where you automatically become a voter when you are old enough, here in America, you need to register first. Federal law allows you to register to vote at the same time you apply for or renew your driver's license in your state. Sixteen states and Washington, D.C., make it even easier by automatically registering you at the time, unless you opt out, and they will update your voter registration whenever you change the address on your driver's license.

How else you can register depends on the state. Many states make it easy to register online. And some states allow you to preregister when you are sixteen or seventeen, meaning that once you turn eighteen you are automatically registered and can vote. Some states will let you register in person on the day of the election, but most have registration deadlines that can be up to thirty days in advance. Organizations like Rock the Vote and Brennan Center for Justice have good overviews of the laws in each state. I know all of you have mad Google skills, so you can easily find the rules on how to register in your state.

But if *you* can't register, much less vote in 2020, why is it important for you to learn about voter registration? Because you can play an important role in making sure everyone you know who *is* eligible is properly registered to vote in this election. If they aren't registered, no matter how strongly they feel about Donald Trump, it really doesn't matter. In order to win, we need everyone who wants a new president to cast a ballot, not just express outrage. And you can't vote if you are not properly registered.

Voter registration is the gateway to the change we all seek.

MAKE SURE YOUR FRIENDS and FAMILY ARE REGISTERED

Make a list of all your friends and family who will be of voting age on November 3, 2020. Contact them all. In person or by phone is best. Ask whether they are registered. If they say yes, great! But ask them to check anyway. If they have moved recently, make sure they know that their data needs to be updated and accurate. You can direct them to websites like iwillvote.com and votesaveamerica.com to find the links to quickly check or change their registration. If any of the people you ask say no, they aren't registered to vote, tell them how important it is to you that they register and vote in this election. Send them to a website like vote.gov, which provides information on how to register in all fifty states, including links to register online for thirty-seven states and the District of Columbia.

AUTOMATIC VOTER REGISTRATION

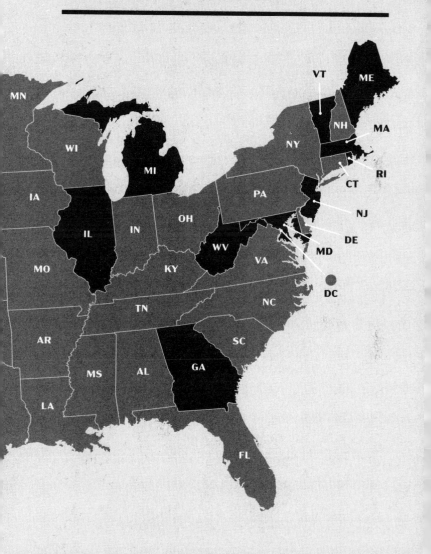

THESE SIXTEEN STATES (AND THE DISTRICT OF COLUMBIA) HAVE APPROVED AUTOMATIC VOTER REGISTRATION.

Check back with your friends and family to make sure they get it done in time.

If you have an older sibling or other relative going to college outside of your home state, and their school happens to be in one of the likely battleground states, encourage them to register where they go to college. It's their right to do so, and we need every vote we can get in states like Wisconsin and Pennsylvania.

Some of the people you are nudging may give you grief. "Why are you asking me? I vote in every election." But most people will be glad you care enough to make sure people in your circle can and will vote. Even if you only help one or two people register, it's a huge deal. This election will probably be super close, so literally every vote counts.

This is an important example of an activity you can participate in that doesn't involve "formal" volunteering. You can do a lot of good going about your daily life, making sure the people you know are registered and have a plan to vote, encouraging them to volunteer, and generally keeping the campaign and the need to be in the fight fully in front of them. If the adults in your life use social media, encourage those who register to post on Facebook or Instagram, perhaps with a quick video explaining why they did it and how easy it was. Even if just one or two people see that and are reminded to register themselves, it's a huge victory.

JOIN A VOTER REGISTRATION DRIVE

You can also volunteer directly to help register people outside your close circle of friends and family.

How would you do this?

First, check on the Democratic nominee's website to see whether there are any volunteer registration activities in your area. It'll be easy to find the volunteer section on the website, and it'll probably ask you to enter your zip code. Your local Democratic Party branch and state and local candidates' offices will also have information on their websites about how to get involved in local registration efforts. Or you can check out websites like mobilizeamerica.io and rockthevote.com, which will also have helpful tips on volunteer registration.

If you live in a battleground state, there are sure to be local registration efforts you, your family, and friends could join. You could sign up to work a voter registration table at a local event—say, a county fair or farmer's market or local festival—where volunteers will have registration forms, tablets, and laptops where people can register to vote right on the spot. It's not much different from setting up a table to sell Girl Scout cookies or candy for a fundraising drive.

Except registering to vote is FREE!

CANVASS

There will probably also be voter registration canvasses. Canvassing means going door to door, trying to contact people directly. You wouldn't do this by yourself. But you and a parent could do it together. And you wouldn't be knocking on just anybody's door. Your local campaign office will organize the canvassing, usually on a weekend, and you and your fellow volunteers will be given lists of citizens in a certain area who are currently not registered but who the campaign believes would almost certainly vote for the Democratic nominee if they were.

Since most adults are already registered to vote, you will not be knocking on every door in a neighborhood. You'll probably knock on one door, and then walk a bit to the next unregistered citizen's door. As a young person, you may have more luck than anyone else in getting these citizens' attention.

I can tell you something about what it is like to do this. You knock on a door, joined by a parent or other family member. If someone answers, you ask for the unregistered citizen by name and hopefully find them at home. Then you might say something like this:

"Hi, I'm Vivian volunteering for the Democratic nominee's campaign. Our records show you are not registered to vote. We could really use your help. Can I help you register?"

If they say yes, depending on the state and the local election laws, you may be able to help them register to vote right there and then. You might have them fill out a form that you take back for the campaign to turn in to election officials, or the campaign may lend you a tablet so the person can register online right on the spot. In some places you may need to leave a registration form for them to complete and send in themselves. Don't worry, you'll be given clear instructions on this step based on the laws in the state.

In some cases the citizen might not want to register. Perhaps the person you are engaging with says something along the lines of, "Thanks, but I just don't see the point. I don't like Trump, but it seems like all the politicians in Washington are terrible. I don't want to decide between the lesser of two evils."

You can craft your own response that is personal to you, and you should if you feel comfortable doing that. An effective generic response, though, could go something like this:

"I totally get that. I'm not old enough to vote yet, and this is the first campaign I've volunteered on. I know the Democrat's not perfect. But my future can't take four more years of Trump. People my age need everyone that *can* vote to do it, so at the very least we can have a president who believes in climate change, won't kick people off health care, and doesn't insult everyone. Maybe you won't end up voting, even though I really hope you do, but will you at least register so you have the choice on Election Day?"

That will be tough to say no to, and you'll put it even better than that.

A young person working hard on behalf of their future can impress even the most cynical person.

And if you do get that person registered, when it comes time to decide whether to vote,

MOST ELIGIBLE VOTERS ARE NEVER ASKED TO REGISTER

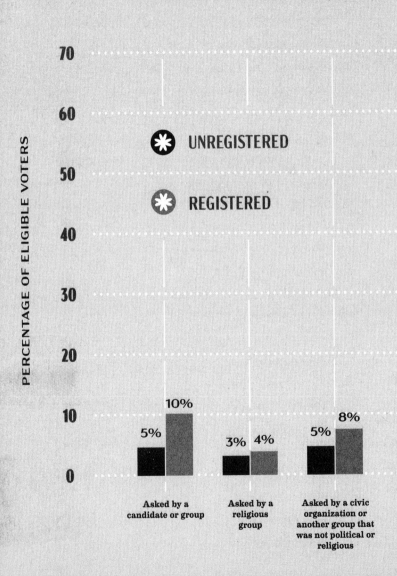

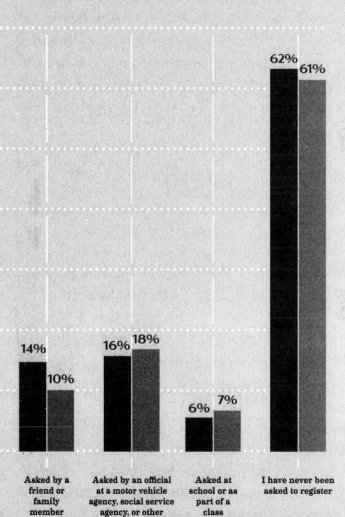

HAVE YOU BEEN ASKED TO REGISTER TO VOTE IN ANY OF THE FOLLOWING WAYS?

14%

10%

16% 18%

6% 7%

62% 61%

Asked by a
friend or
family
member

Asked by an official
at a motor vehicle
agency, social service
agency, or other
government office

Asked at
school or as
part of a
class

I have never been
asked to register

Note: Respondents could select more than one answer.

they most likely won't be thinking about the debates, if they watched them, or advertisements or whatever story they saw in their Facebook feed. They will be thinking about you. And your future. And not wanting to let you down. It's a twofold win you've accomplished. You have encouraged them to register, and that exchange has stuck with them, inspiring them to cast their ballot to defeat Trump.

If the person who answers the next door isn't interested in talking, or is rude to you, try not to take it personally. It will happen, human beings being human beings. Maybe they are having a bad day or just hate politics. Shake it off, on to the next door. You'll also knock on a lot of doors where people aren't home or don't answer.

That's okay. Maybe you'll only convince one or two people to register, and this may seem like a lot of work for a seemingly small outcome, but remember there will be thousands more like you doing the same thing. It all adds up, and fast.

Registering eligible voters in battleground states will have the biggest impact, but even if you don't live in a battleground state and can't travel to one, there are still important ways you can help on voter registration efforts.

JOIN A PHONE BANK

The Democratic presidential campaign, your local Democratic Party branch, and progressive groups like NextGen America, Swing Left, and Indivisible will have information on their websites about phone banks you may be able to take part in. Phone banks are opportunities for volunteers to get together and call people who are voter registration priorities in the battleground states. You don't have to be on the ground in a battleground state to make a phone call, but just like when you knock on a door, you can make a strong pitch that might make all the difference and convince someone to register to vote.

For a phone banking event, just as for door-to-door canvassing, the Democratic campaign will provide lists of unregistered eligible voters who the campaign believes would vote for their candidate. Even though most of the people you call won't answer, when people respond and say they will register, you get to celebrate that good news with your fellow volunteers. It's inspiring and fun to do this work alongside others who are fighting for the same cause.

A phone call is probably not as effective as knocking on a door because an in-person conversation is usually longer and has the benefit of being face-to-face. And you won't be there to help the person register or fill out forms on the spot. But we won't reach everyone through canvassing neighborhoods, and the person-to-person contact you can have on the phone is still much better and potentially more effective than a digital ad or piece of mail these same citizens will be sent to encourage them to register.

The person on the other end of the phone, just like someone who sees you at the door, may pick up on the fact that you are younger and ask you about it. This can be another great opportunity to express in your own authentic, passionate voice why you are so involved in this election and what it means to your future.

A major focus of voter registration efforts will be aimed at people who aren't registered in presidential battlegrounds, but the impact of registering more voters will be felt in races up and down the ballot, not just in the presidential election. Your efforts can help Democrats win races for the Senate and House, governor, and state legislature too.

Even if you don't live in a presidential battleground, you can join important local efforts to help elect good Democrats who will serve as important allies in Congress and at the state level if we are successful in electing a Democratic president in 2020. These new, exciting young candidates will become future leaders in the party. Maybe even president one day.

While registering voters in California, New York, or South Carolina may not affect the presidential outcome, it can make a difference in important elections in those states. No matter where it happens, it feels awfully good to witness an unregistered voter, who could not or did not fully participate in their democracy, turning into a participant. Change happens one person at a time, one vote at a time, and you're making sure more people have the opportunity to be part of that change.

GET CREATIVE

I am constantly amazed at what my children create. Their friends too. Videos, drawings, poems, stories, pictures, songs. They express their hopes and dreams so much more inventively than I could ever imagine doing.

What if thousands, perhaps tens of thousands, of young people your age turned some of those creative juices toward getting people motivated to participate and vote in the 2020 election?

It would be incredibly powerful and inspiring, and it could help elect a new president. It would also be authentic and from the heart.

When a presidential campaign or the Democratic Party puts out videos, social media posts, or written statements, they are seen as propaganda, even by people who are most passionate about the cause. Official messaging can come across as marketing, and it can seem self-serving. It isn't much different from corporate advertising. Even if the advertising is clever, you may still wonder how much you can believe it. What else are they going to say other than their product is awesome and life changing?

But when average people lift up their voices and find creative ways to advocate for a cause, it can cut through the noise. It's more believable, and people will be more interested in the content because it was made by people like them, people they can relate to.

I think this is even more true when young people step out and step up and use their voices on behalf of causes they believe in.

A heartfelt message from a young person will reach people around their same age, but older people will also be curious about, and perhaps inspired by, a young person who cares so much that they took the time to create a piece of original content to advocate for something they believe in.

A lot of adults have become cynical about politicians and the media, but they still believe kids.

What you say can jolt us out of our routines and make us stop and think for a minute about what we are doing and why.

In the presidential campaign, there are a gazillion ways you can use your creative talents to motivate others.

I'm sure you'll have even better ideas than I do, but I'll give you a few examples of some things you might try and why I think they matter. Before we get into that, though, I need to add one important note. Social media and the internet can be incredible tools for connecting with others and spreading messages that are important to you, but there are dark sides to these tools, and every family will have their own rules about using the internet. You must have the permission and guidance of your parents or guardians before engaging online or via social media.

DOCUMENT YOUR EXPERIENCE

If you and your family and friends are going out to do some volunteer canvassing, capture that in a video. Make it fun and informative. Show people what it's like to arrive at the campaign office, provide commentary on some of the great conversations you had with voters, capture the elation your mom feels after convincing someone to vote.

At the end, perhaps you deliver a message that tells people you had a great time and you think it made a difference. Ask people to try volunteering themselves.

With your parents' permission, share the video on the networks you use. Or ask them to share it. Then others will share it from there and your message can spread.

You'll almost certainly convince a bunch of your friends to volunteer too, and they will get *their* family and friends to try volunteering as well.

Think about the power of that. The canvassing you and your crew did in and of itself is incredibly important. Hopefully you helped put some votes in the bank for our nominee. But now, because you captured the experience, you are the reason many *more* people will go out and make the same difference you did.

You've found a way to amplify your good efforts and help the campaign gather enough volunteers to do the work required to win.

SHARE THE ISSUES THAT MATTER TO YOU

Another idea would be for you to make a series of short videos where you talk about why this election is so important to you and what specific issues motivated you to get involved even though you can't vote yet.

Maybe the first one is on climate change. You can explain that time is running out to save the planet and that if we have four more years of a president who doesn't believe in climate change and is doing things to make it worse, the future for you and your generation will be bleak. You can say why you believe electing a new president is possibly our last, best hope to do what is required to bend the curve on carbon emissions and give the planet a chance. Of course, you should put your own feelings in your own words and talk about the aspects of climate change and the environment that matter most to you. These are just some ideas for inspiration.

Maybe you end by asking people to share your video and make their own. Or maybe you ask other young people to get involved if they believe, as you do, that this is the critical moment to save our planet. Tell them to ask their friends and family to get involved as well.

Your climate video could have a bigger impact on the people who see it than a speech from our nominee or any scientific article or celebrities' social media posts. That's because your message comes from a regular person, someone like them. Someone whose future is at stake, someone who uses the same words and has the same thoughts and feelings they do.

And perhaps most important, from someone who is taking action, who is getting into the fight. If you can do it, so can they.

You can follow your first video with other videos that speak to other reasons why you are so passionate about electing a new president. If you speak from your own experience, about the issues that matter to you and your family, your videos will move the people who see them. Maybe one of your parents lost a job due to Trump's trade and tariff wars. You might speak about that searing experience, what it has done to your family, and why we need a change.

Perhaps you have a relative with a serious, preexisting health condition, and the Trump administration is putting them in danger of losing their health care coverage. You can capture how frightening it is to live on the edge, and how all that fear will go away if we elect a new president who is committed to protecting people.

Maybe you or your family members have experienced racial discrimination. You might speak about what's it like to grow up in a country where you worry that discrimination is getting even worse.

Maybe you have a friend whose parents are undocumented. You can educate people on what it's like for your friend to live in constant fear that today is the day their parents get deported.

Whatever issues motivate you, speak about as many as you can.

Each time you do, you will reach different people. It may make them more certain to vote. It could provide the push to get them more involved as a volunteer.

It will also just feel really good to speak out and articulate your feelings and explain why you are so invested in electing a new president. And those videos will live forever, so when you are older and have kids of your own and they ask what it was like to live through this time, you can show them. You can inspire them with your story of how, at one of America's lowest moments, you had the courage to stand up and fight for a better tomorrow for our country and for kids like them.

DRAW! WRITE! SING!

There are so many ways to use your creative talents to make a difference. Perhaps you like to draw. Draw a picture of what you imagine it will be like on election night when it is announced that your candidate has won. Maybe that's a picture of your family celebrating around a television in your living room. Perhaps it's a picture of young people celebrating together in your backyard. Maybe it's a picture of the sun rising high into the sky. Whatever comes to mind, share that drawing, or ask your parents to share it on their social media channels. Maybe your caption says something like, "Want this night to happen? Only if you work hard for it." You or your parents can include a link about how to volunteer. Your art and your call for people to work hard will inspire some people who had not thought about volunteering to do so.

Do you like to write poetry? Write a poem about the election, or about a specific issue you care about, and like the drawing idea above, share it. It could make a big impact.

Maybe you and your family will want to participate in a march or make a statement at a local event. Get some of your friends together to create homemade signs about the issues that motivate you. "Save the Planet, Vote Democratic." "Protect Children, Not Guns." "Vote for My Future." You'll have your own ideas, and they'll be good ones.

Those signs and messages will reach people who see them in person, but people will also take pictures at the event and share with their networks. Maybe you live in Manchester, Iowa, but someone your age in Manchester, New Hampshire, could see the pictures of you and your sign and get motivated to become more heavily involved.

Maybe you and your friends who play in a band together decide to write and record a song about your feelings about the election. One of your parents can record you performing it and release it out in the wild. Maybe it even goes viral. That song can reach people of all ages and speak to them in a way that more "official" channels never will.

In 2008, at a crucial point in Obama's presidential campaign, the artist will.i.am gathered other musicians and celebrities and crafted a song and video around the words and footage from one of Obama's speeches. The video was viewed and shared millions and millions and millions of times and caused many new donors and volunteers to join our campaign. And back in 2008 social networks and video sharing were just getting started! If you google "Yes We Can will.i.am," you can find and watch the video for inspiration. You don't need famous musicians and celebrities to create something wonderful.

Just bring your passion and your talents.

Each time you have an interesting thought about the election or when you volunteer or watch important moments like the conventions and debates, take a moment to think about whether there is something you can do creatively to capture what you're feeling. A young person honestly sharing their experience will always be interesting to others. At the very least, it will be a healthy outlet for you to express yourself. But it might do far more than that. It might be the reason some people get more involved or more committed to voting.

And if enough of you are doing it, you can reach enough people to make a real difference in this election.

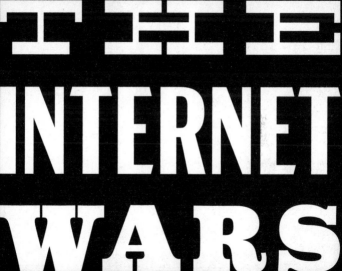

THE
INTERNET
WARS

HOW COMMUNICATION HAS CHANGED CAMPAIGNS

A long time ago, political campaigns used to be fought in town squares and in newspapers. Candidates gave speeches in cities where just about everybody showed up, and newspapers, many of them politically affiliated with one side or the other, lifted up their preferred candidate and blasted the ones they opposed.

Then radio became the main arena for political communication, with Franklin Delano Roosevelt perfecting the craft with his fireside radio chats. By the 1960s television took over, perhaps most famously in 1960, when John F. Kennedy won a tight race in large part because in the first televised presidential debate in American history, JFK looked young and vigorous and confident while his opponent,

Richard Nixon, looked ill and pasty and sweaty. The makeup Nixon used to cover his growing stubble melted under the lights.

Kennedy's team made sure he was clean-shaven and would look good under the television studio lighting. Kennedy and his team understood that the debate was as much about how you looked and presented yourself as what you said. I wish that were not the case, and I'm afraid too much attention is still paid to presentation, especially and unfairly if you are a female candidate. But back then, seeing both candidates live on a television screen was a novelty, and the importance of appearance was amplified.

It has been reported that those who listened to the debate on the radio judged Nixon the winner. If only he had shaved right before the debate instead of hours before in the morning, and had taken how he looked a bit more seriously, it's quite possible he would have won the presidential election that year. The margins were so close, with Kennedy winning Hawaii by just 115 votes, and Missouri and Illinois, two big states, by less than ten thousand votes.

By 2008, when I was managing Barack Obama's campaign, the internet was growing in importance. We ran the first presidential campaign to really think internet first. Back then, that primarily meant using our website to recruit donors and volunteers, advertise online, and put videos on the barackobama.com YouTube channel. (It's still around, check it out!) We built our own social media site that supporters could use to find each other and volunteer together in their community, even before any official campaign staff were on the ground.

FACEBOOK

We had to create our own network because in 2008 Facebook was just beginning to be used outside of college campuses, where the company started. Twitter was still new and was not yet heavily used. Instagram wasn't invented yet and neither was Snapchat or TikTok.

So while we did all we could to utilize the internet to get our message out and recruit and motivate our millions of volunteers, the old media of television, radio, and newspapers were still critical, and we spent a lot of time and money making sure we were using them to full advantage.

By our reelection campaign in 2012, things had shifted dramatically. Facebook was now how many Americans communicated with each other and received and shared information. And Twitter, while not a network most Americans were on, was where almost all the political journalists and political insiders spent a lot of time, so it was an important filter for the messages we were trying to get out. Our campaign changed accordingly, focusing even more of our strategy and tactics on the web and social media.

By 2016, Facebook was the main arena the campaign was fought in. While statistics show (and you and your friends may fall into this category) that fewer young people are signing up for Facebook in favor of other social media sites, the vast majority of likely voters in America have a Facebook account, and they log in and spend time on the site.

The Trump campaign was a Facebook-first campaign in 2016. The Clinton campaign spent a lot of resources there as well, but most experts thought Trump did a better job using the platform to persuade voters and find supporters. And as you may have heard, Russia decided to weaponize Facebook to influence the election, creating fake ads to sow division and help Trump win.

THE DIGITAL WAR IN 2020

In the 2020 election, the internet will be more important than ever. In the previous chapter we talked about how the content you create can be powerfully distributed online and via social media (with the permission and guidance of your parents or guardians). But you won't be able to put out those messages every day. Yet every day, in fact every second, a digital war is being fought between Trump and his opponents to get their messages out, both positive and negative. They will be trying to motivate their own side and discourage the other side.

The campaigns and their allies will spend billions of dollars on these efforts, and they have very sophisticated data about the people they should be sending specific advertisements and content to.

Hearing this may make you ask, What does it have to do with me? How can one person, a young person without a vote no less, compete against that wall of money and relentless activity? Shouldn't our nominee be able to take care of these things on their own, since they will have a lot of resources and expertise?

These are fair questions, but the truth is that if enough of us don't jump into the digital fray every day, Trump will have a significant advantage, which will help him win.

First, Trump and his allies will have more money than our side. Second, as foreign interference was a factor in the last presidential election, we can expect it to happen again. And third, the political right has allies in the Fox News television network, conservative radio hosts, and right-wing websites that get a lot of traffic. All these outlets will constantly be putting out misinformation and worse about the Democratic nominee—all material that gets turned into shareable content by Trump supporters across the internet.

The Democrats do not have a similarly powerful and consistent constellation of media properties that are coordinated and focused, day in and day out, on reaching the masses. So, we have less money, no foreign assistance, and no huge and coordinated message network.

How on earth can we compete?

What do we have that can make any difference at all?

OUR WEAPONS

We have two things: the truth and you. We need millions of Americans, even tens of millions of Americans, fighting back against the misinformation and helping our candidate get their ideas and plans out. We don't have to lie, and we don't have to do anything sleazy.

We just have to get in the game.

As I've said before, every family has their own rules and norms around the use of social media. You may be too young to have your own account, or your parents may not allow it. If they do allow you to use social media independently, you should still have their permission and guidance before you post. And yes, you can participate in this fight even if your family won't let you anywhere near your own social media account. You may not have an account, but I bet your parents or other adult family members do. You can get those family members on board and coach them on how to use social media to spread truth.

LEAD YOUR OWN DIGITAL ARMY

First, you can make sure your adult family and friends who are committed to beating Trump are ready to do their part. Talk to each of them and ask what digital accounts they have. YouTube? Facebook? Instagram? Twitter? TikTok? If they don't have any, encourage them to sign up. If they grumble, remind them that they can get rid of the accounts after the election.

Once you have them on board, talk to them about how they are using their accounts. My hunch is that most are not using them frequently enough, or smartly enough, and some not at all in terms of helping us win the election.

You may already know a lot more about how to use these sites effectively than your older friends and family members. You've grown up as digital natives, and it's natural and intuitive to most of you. You can be the guide and director of your own content network if you get a few (or many!) people committed to sharing helpful content throughout the election.

SPREAD POSITIVE MESSAGES

The first thing we all need to do is help get our nominee's own positive message and ideas for the country out to voters all across America. This is incredibly important for a few reasons. First, the media will not spend much time covering ideas and policies. Sadly, the media will focus on the polling in the race and who is ahead or behind. And as important and rarely used as impeachment is in our system, we know the wall-to-wall attention on that process will dwarf our candidate's plans to fight climate change or pay teachers more. If history is any guide, the latest Trump tweet will get a million times more coverage than our candidate's plans to make college more affordable.

On top of all that, the Trump campaign and its allies are likely to spend hundreds of millions of dollars on online advertising, including trying to distort what our candidate would do as president. They may say things like our candidate does not believe murderers should be in prison, or will raise taxes on everyone in America, or won't take care of veterans. They may even try to convince young people that our candidate will be bad on climate change, just to confuse and distort. Their hope in all of this is to discourage people, causing them not to vote or volunteer.

You can counteract this misinformation when you help create content that captures why you believe in our candidate. You'll know how to amplify what you like about our candidate: their leadership and character and their plans and positions on the issues you care about. And you will know how to distill these points into shareable bites—the best thing to share on social media.

You can also help discover compelling content bouncing around the internet. It could be an excerpt of a speech our candidate gives on climate change promising to rejoin the Paris Climate Agreement. (Trump withdrew the United States from this international agreement to fight global warming.) Or maybe it's a clip of our candidate promising to find a solution to the gun violence in our country.

If you find something that moves you, share it, or get your network of adults to share it.

BE BOLD AND HOPEFUL

You may wonder, "Hey, this is a presidential candidate giving an important speech on an important topic. Won't most people see it, and won't I annoy them if I share it or get my parents to?"

Nope and nope.

Big nope and nope.

It's really hard to reach people in today's fragmented media and digital universe. So, odds are they didn't see it or only vaguely heard about it. But even if they have already seen it,

the fact that you or someone in your circle felt strongly enough to share that our candidate's words resonated with you will be interesting to others and may motivate them.

Every day the Democratic presidential campaign and its allies will produce videos, infographics, and written content that makes the positive case on issues like health care, climate and the environment, taxes, student loans, gun safety, and foreign policy. And there will be tons of news articles that will analyze and capture the value of what our candidate is proposing.

We need millions of Americans to share positive and motivational content they see and like with their social networks. You can help make sure all the adults you know who are committed to this fight are set up and actively using the internet, email, and social media to full effect.

You can create content to share with them, and you can find content created by others that inspires you. Keep your networks sharing positive material that supports our candidate as widely as possible. And when you do, it would be great if you included a link that people can use to sign up to volunteer.

Using the Paris Climate Agreement example,

you could post a clip of the most powerful part of our candidate's speech, along with a caption that says something like "This election is about the future of our planet. Sign up to help us save it." Then include a link to the page on our candidate's website where volunteers can join the fight.

In the lead-up to the election, when friends or family members say they saw something that excited them about our candidate, you might say, "That's great. How did you share it?" If they say they didn't think to share, stay on them until they do.

We don't have the luxury in this election of not spreading the word, assuming someone else will, or thinking that the campaign will take care of everything.

We all have to take responsibility for making sure everyone knows why we think

the Democratic candidate will do good things for them, the country, and the world.

Spreading all the reasons we're excited about our next president and what they will do is the fun part. And sharing why we think Trump has been a bad president and why America can't afford four more years of him can also be effective—there is no shortage of reasons and material, for one thing. The prospect of what he will continue to do with another term as president can provide a lot of the motivation we need to give this election all we have.

But we have to get people as excited to vote *for* something as *against*.

The arguments you and all of us will make on behalf of the Democratic nominee are grounded in truth. Facts. Math. Our candidate will have a plan to provide better access to health care and will make fighting climate change the number-one priority. They will raise taxes on the rich to lift up those working hard to escape poverty and strengthen those in the middle class struggling to stay there. Our candidate will get us back in the Iran nuclear deal, lessening the threat of war, and strengthen our alliances instead of embracing dictators and despots, as Trump has done.

FIGHTING BACK

But there is another task we have to take on, one that might be less fun and one that I wish was not an aspect of the democratic process. A big part of the 2020 campaign will turn on whether we can fight back effectively against the false narratives and disinformation campaigns that are certain to play a major role in this election cycle.

If the Trump campaign can create a negative impression of the Democratic nominee, distorting both who they are and what they believe in, it will do so in the hope that it might turn voters off. This strategy is less about getting voters committed to voting for Trump and more about getting them not to vote at all, or hoping they will vote for a third-party candidate in protest against both mainstream candidates. If this happens, it essentially reduces the number of votes Trump needs to get to win.

In the 2016 election, Trump only got 46.1 percent of the vote nationally, and not much more than that in key battleground states like Michigan, Wisconsin, and Pennsylvania.

It's hard to see Trump getting to 50 percent or even 49 percent in the key states he needs to win. So his strategy will be to make the Democratic candidate so unappealing to certain voters that even though they may not like Trump, they decide they can't vote for the Democrat.

He might say the Democrat is going to raise taxes on every American and make it harder for people to get health care. He may tell people that the Democratic candidate wants no border security and will let violent criminals run free.

He could criticize our nominee personally, maybe on ethics, maybe on finances, maybe on their gender or race or appearance.

One of the most dangerous things the Trump campaign and its allies are likely to do is create content and send messages aimed directly at younger voters to confuse them. They may use social media advertisements to create the impression that the Democratic candidate won't do anything about climate change. Or that the Democratic candidate is anti-immigrant. Or that our candidate will make it harder and more expensive to get student loans.

IS IT FAKE NEWS?

WHEN YOU SEE STORIES ONLINE THAT YOU AREN'T SURE ABOUT, HERE ARE SOME STEPS YOU CAN TAKE AND QUESTIONS YOU CAN ASK.

CHECK OUT THE WEBSITE

What site is publishing the story?
What is their stated mission?
What other articles are on the site?

LOOK INTO THE AUTHOR

Research the author's name online.
Is this a real person?
Is this a credible writer?

IS THIS A NEW STORY?

Sometimes old stories are dug up and republished. It can be misleading to make something that happened long ago appear to be a recent event.

INVESTIGATE YOUR BIAS

We all have beliefs. Sometimes, we are more likely to believe stories that tend to confirm what we already think.

LOOK PAST THE HEADLINES

Does the story support the assertion of the headline? Clickbait headlines can be misleading.

WHAT ARE THE SOURCES?

Credible journalism will cite sources. Click through to the links and investigate where the story comes from.

IS THIS MEANT TO BE FUNNY?

A very outrageous story might be someone's attempt at a joke. Look into the author and the site to see if this might be the case.

ASK FOR HELP

Discuss the story with a parent, a teacher, or a librarian. Or try a fact-checking site.

Of course, the Democratic candidate's position is likely to be just the opposite. But the opposition will be betting that some people will see this information and get discouraged. And they know that this type of content will be shared aggressively by Trump supporters on social media and in email chains.

Those attacks would be so outrageously false, you might think, who would believe them? Why waste time worrying about such nonsense?

Well, even if one person believed them and decided not to vote, or to vote for a third-party candidate, it's one too many. And recent history shows us that we need to be concerned. These tactics could have a much bigger impact.

LESSONS FROM RECENT CAMPAIGNS

Back in 2016, there were attacks bouncing around the internet saying that the Democratic candidate, Hillary Clinton, was part of secret crime rings, that she had undisclosed health problems and didn't have the stamina to be president, that she would soon be indicted for all her alleged "crimes." Why bother voting for her if she was going to jail and would never be sworn in as our president? I made the mistake of thinking no one would believe this crazy stuff, and I know a lot of others did too.

We can't make that mistake again. The disinformation machine will be much more sophisticated and dangerous in 2020 than it was in 2016.

What can you do about it? Well first, if you see any of your friends or family sharing any of these false narratives, try to shut them down with the truth right away.

Whether it's in person, in a group text, or on social media, if someone you know talks or posts about one of the stories you know to be untrue, it's time to get to work.

Let's say a friend of one of your older siblings, who is eighteen and can vote, states, "I'm worried that the Democratic candidate will make it more expensive to go to college. They want to make it more expensive to get loans." The worst thing to do is not respond at all. And the next worst thing is to brush it off with "That's ridiculous." We need to take all these stories seriously because they could take root.

You should craft a response that feels natural to you. But something like this might be helpful: "Do you really think a Democratic candidate would run on making it harder to go to college? They want to make it *easier* for everyone. They want to make sure it's affordable!"

In addition to fighting back with the facts on whatever crazy stories we hear, be prepared to see doctored video and audio in the campaign that will confuse even the most digitally savvy people. It's critically important to remind people of *this* truth—that distorting the truth to confuse people *is* the strategy.

If we can get enough people to believe in and remember that important fact, they will begin to look more skeptically on their own at potential disinformation.

Just as you've mobilized your friends and family networks to make sure they are properly registered, know how to volunteer, and are using their social media platforms to spread the truth, you need to push them to fight back against false narratives as well.

Your first job is to convince them it's important. Every time you hear or see someone in your family exasperatedly complaining about an untrue story, quickly ask, "What are you going to do about it? Because someone may hear it and think it's true, and if enough people believe this stuff, Trump will win again."

It would also be smart to encourage your friends and family to expand their networks on Facebook, Twitter, and Instagram. Ask them to be sure they are following all their friends and relatives on social media. Because doing so enables them to see what *others* are seeing. With your help, they will be able to respond to the nonsense when they see it, as well as amplify our nominee's positive vision and ideas.

Some people won't be comfortable responding to disinformation in their own words. That's okay. You can help them quickly find content to counteract it that they can link to or paste and share in social media feeds or email chains.

Way back in 2007 and 2008, which may seem like the dark ages to some of you, Barack Obama was facing a barrage of disinformation. Back then, which was before social media had really large numbers of users, the primary way these attacks were shared was on long email chains, where people would share false "content" about our soon-to-be forty-fourth president.

At first, we thought no one we really cared about electorally would believe any of it. A lot of the stories centered on the idea that Obama was not a "real" American because his father was from Africa, or they claimed that he went to radical schools when he lived in Indonesia as a boy and was trained to hate America. Others said that Obama lied about being a Christian or that he loved terrorist groups like al-Qaeda. (Osama bin Laden certainly wishes that were true!) We at campaign headquarters were slow to understand how dangerous these assertions can become when they go unanswered.

But our campaign workers in the battleground states were starting to get asked about these crazy stories. Our own supporters and volunteers, who knew how nuts this stuff was, were getting questions about it when they tried to recruit other supporters and volunteers. The disinformation was spreading so widely that it got to the point where voters were even asking Barack Obama himself about it when he was out campaigning. We decided, much later than we should have, that we had to get serious about fighting back. And most important, we had to find ways to arm our staff and volunteers with easy-to-find material to push back on these nasty email chains as well as to deal with the disinformation when it came up in conversation.

In June 2008, just as the general election was starting against Senator John McCain, we launched a website specifically to fight back. On the site we actually listed every attack and smear about Barack Obama that we knew was bouncing around the internet and into email in-boxes. It was quite unorthodox for a campaign to list the attacks against its candidate. But we wanted to make it easy for our volunteers to find what they were looking for. On the site we provided rebuttal information—news articles, videos, our own talking points, whatever we had that our supporters could grab a link to and attach to an email or share with a questioning voter.

If it had been just our campaign staff making the rebuttals, countering all the false narratives would have been an impossible game of whack-a-mole. We'd never have been able to keep up. But because of our passionate volunteers, including a lot of young people helping in the effort, we had millions trying to take a hammer and bop down the disinformation as it reared its head.

LOOKING FORWARD

In 2020, we need our nominee to modernize this approach. The campaign will need to have an awesomely simple menu of content on its website, categorized by issue or attack, that lets supporters find, copy, and share effective responses in seconds. Even better would be an app designed for this sole purpose, since so much of this campaign will be battled on smartphones. I hope our nominee will quickly put these tools in place. When the rebuttal information does appear, show your family and friends the website and make sure they download any helpful apps.

Responding to disinformation is difficult enough. If it takes too much time, that's a double whammy and a lot of people won't do it, not even our candidate's most committed supporters. Our candidate needs their positive message to reach everyone it can. Help make the case for them by making sure the inevitable false narratives don't take hold and hurt the Democrat's ability to win.

There is no magical cavalry out there or set of responsible referees to make things right.

Only we can do it. So we must. Because so many of you are more digitally savvy than your elders and are great at research and finding nuggets of information and content, you can help lead the way for the rest of us.

7

MONEY

PRESIDENTIAL CANDIDATES LEGITIMATELY
need to raise a lot of money. A lot. There
will be billions spent in this presidential
election. Some of that will be silly spending
by outside groups that won't be effective. But
our nominee's campaign will need to make
sure it has enough financial resources to do
everything required to get to 270 electoral
votes and win the presidency.

In both of Barack Obama's campaigns,
we were blessed by the generosity and
commitment of millions of Americans who
made sure we had the money to invest and
innovate pretty much everywhere we needed
to. It might seem like a luxury, but actually
it's a necessity given the stakes. To know all
the things you need to do to win and not be
able to do them because the campaign can't
afford it is tragic.

WHAT DOES IT GET SPENT ON?

So, what does a presidential campaign need enough money to do? Hire staff, ultimately thousands of people, to work on the campaign, for one. And it takes money to raise money, so you need to invest heavily in digital, phone, and mail solicitations to build your donor list. You need to be campaigning all over the country, so you have to pay for travel—planes, hotels, ride shares, rental cars—for the candidate, their family, and the staff who travel.

Campaigns are businesses, so you have all the expenses you might expect—legal fees, credit card processing fees, insurance, office rentals, computers, servers, office furniture, and supplies. The bulk of the spending, however, occurs in the battleground states. Advertising, signs, state staff, local office space, materials for volunteers to use—the list goes on and on. Each state will have a financial budget, based on what the campaign thinks is required to win, as well as a people budget—how many active volunteers will be required to register, persuade, and turn out the target voters. Florida will be much more expensive, given its size, than Wisconsin, and Texas will be the biggest battleground state of all if it is hotly contested in 2020.

But a presidential campaign cannot target more states than it has money for. It would be historically tragic if the campaign thought our nominee could compete vigorously in eight to ten states and possibly win, but didn't end up targeting some because there wasn't enough money. The fewer states you target, the smaller margin for error you have. We need to ensure our nominee does not have to make strategic retreats that could cost the presidency due to a lack of funding.

CAN I CONTRIBUTE?

Now, does that mean you should collect your birthday money and the money you've made babysitting or mowing lawns and contribute it all to the campaign? Maybe. You are allowed to contribute at your age, as long as it's your own money. So if it's a choice between more Fortnite skins or giving some money to a cause you believe in, do the right thing.

But if you are saving up money to pay for college or you're helping support your family, then no. A hard no on that. The truth is our candidate has plenty of people who have the resources and financial security to give without putting undue pressure on those who don't. The last point is important. If your family is struggling financially, do not suggest that your parents find a way to contribute money. Your time, passion, and creativity are more than enough contribution to the campaign. Others who can give without major sacrifice need to step up and make sure the campaign has the funding to win.

If you come from a family that you think could afford to help the campaign financially, have the conversation with your parents and other family members. You can help them understand why it's important, what the money will be spent on and where, and how our candidate will get outspent by Trump and the conservative money machine. Maybe you talk about trade-offs. If the family gives $250 or $500, it may mean a shorter vacation or eating out less often. Maybe those small sacrifices are okay to make. Each family is different and you know yours best. But trade-offs between basic necessities like clothes, food, or rent and a donation to the campaign are never okay.

If your family agrees that they want to and can afford to contribute, talk about the best way to do it. You could give your maximum contribution right away, online. Presto, a few taps on keyboard or phone, and the money is being put to work to defeat Trump. Maybe it's easier for your family to sign up for a smaller monthly amount, so you don't have to give a large amount up front. Perhaps your family would like to attend an event, to meet others supporting our candidate and be motivated by that fellowship. No matter where you live, there will be an event you could attend. Our candidate will speak at some events in larger cities. The candidate's family members, leading Democratic officials, and athletes and celebrities will speak at events as well. In smaller, less populated areas it could be an event with the Democratic state senator. The point is that if you don't just want to give online, you can find some live events you can give to.

Just as every vote counts, every dollar counts.

Some families can give $2,500 without breaking a sweat. For others, $25 is the absolute max. Both donations matter, and if anything, the $25 contribution means more because it was likely harder to give. Time and money are both incredibly precious commodities for most people in America. To win this campaign, we'll need people to give what they can of both, but without harming their families and future.

FUNDRAISING

You've probably been involved in fundraising efforts before, maybe with a 5K run for a certain cause or a candy sale to benefit your school. You and your friends and family may want to think of a fundraising activity that you can do on behalf of the Democratic nominee. You can use your skills and creativity to help raise some of the money our candidate will need to build a winning campaign.

Maybe you and your family can have a yard sale. Clear out the toys you no longer play with and the clothes that no longer fit and donate the money you make to our nominee's campaign. If you and your friends love to make cupcakes or cookies, have a bake sale to raise money. Or an art and poetry sale if those are your talents. Or a battle of the bands. Let people know what you're doing it for and why you care. Your genuine passion will be even harder to resist than a cupcake.

8

GO
O
GET   OUT
TV
THE   VOTE!

WHAT DOES THIS ACRONYM MEAN?

Game of Thrones viewers?

Grind out the victory?

Neither, but in politics, its actual meaning comes closer to the latter.

Get out the vote.

Getting out the vote is an incredibly important part of any campaign. As much as we wish it were otherwise, at the end of the day, despite all the hard work to get them on the rolls, a lot of *registered* voters won't cast their votes. Over seventy-seven million registered voters did not vote in 2016. That's on top of the nearly seventeen million citizens who were eligible to vote but did not register.

VOTER TURNOUT

It's likely we will have a higher voter turnout in 2020 than we have seen in some time. Donald Trump will help drive turnout on both sides in all parts of the country. A lot of people in this country believe that Trump is protecting them and the things they care about. And they want four more years of it. They will vote in droves. And if you are reading this book, you probably know how passionate so many people on our side are. A lot of people in this country feel just as strongly that Trump should not win reelection. They will turn out too.

VOTER TURNOUT IN MIDTERM ELECTIONS

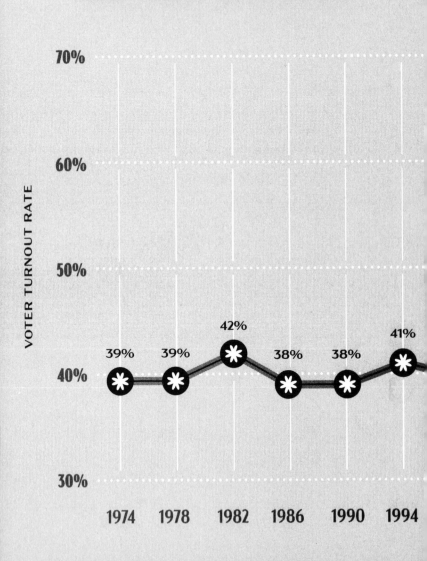

VOTER TURNOUT AS A PERCENTAGE OF VOTING-ELIGIBLE POPULATION

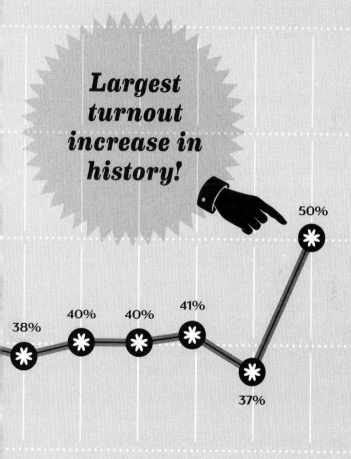

Largest turnout increase in history!

50%

38% 40% 40% 41%

37%

1998 2002 2006 2010 2014 2018

LEARNING FROM THE 2018 ELECTIONS

We saw an important signal about how high turnout could go in 2018. It was the highest turnout for a midterm congressional election—when there is no presidential race on the ballot—since 1914. 1914! Almost all the political observers thought we'd never see turnout that high again, largely because they thought many younger voters in particular would only vote in presidential elections. Well, two years ago younger voters proved the naysayers wrong. Some of them may have been your older siblings or cousins. Voters under thirty turned out in record numbers and voted Democratic by historic margins.

Democrats won over forty U.S. House seats and returned the Speaker's gavel to Nancy Pelosi. Few thought this would be possible for the Democrats. Democrats also won hundreds of state legislative seats. They won back the governor's offices in Michigan and Wisconsin and came within a whisker in Georgia and Florida.

The U.S. Senate races could have been a bloodbath for Democrats. But losses were held to a minimum. We won seats in Nevada and Arizona and only narrowly lost in surprising places like Texas.

Given the outcome, it's clear the record turnout helped Democrats across the board. But Republican turnout was strong as well, helping the GOP win a number of key Senate races. Donald Trump implored his supporters to vote in the midterm elections, and many of them heeded the call even though he was not on the ballot. He is most definitely on the ballot in 2020. We had better assume that every Trump supporter in America, and pretty much every conservative voter, is coming out to vote. Republicans historically vote more reliably than Democrats. We have to work harder to make sure we get our vote out too.

YOUNGER GENERATIONS OUTVOTED OLDER GENERATIONS IN 2018

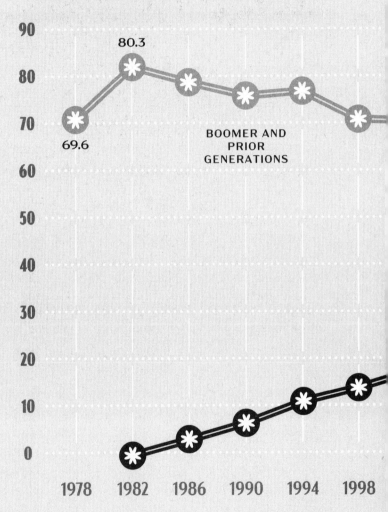

VOTES (IN MILLONS)

90

80.3

80

70

69.6

BOOMER AND
PRIOR
GENERATIONS

60

50

40

30

20

10

0

1978 1982 1986 1990 1994 1998

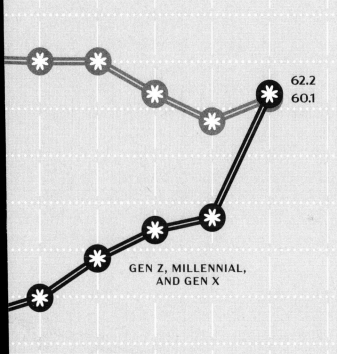

62.2
60.1

GEN Z, MILLENNIAL,
AND GEN X

2002   2006   2010   2014   2018

YOU CAN GOTV WHEREVER YOU ARE

So, Democrats should gain more from a huge turnout than the GOP. But we are going to have to work incredibly hard to make sure that happens. And it's important that we get the higher turnout where we need it. While it will help Democrats up and down the ballot to get awesome turnout in California and New York, we need to make sure we get jaw-dropping turnout in Wisconsin, Michigan, and North Carolina too. Hillary Clinton lost the presidency in part because turnout in Detroit, Michigan, and Milwaukee, Wisconsin, two predominantly Democratic areas, was way below Obama's turnout. We can't let that happen again. And you can help make sure it doesn't.

First, go back to the lists you made of your friends and family for volunteering and registration and social networking. Ask people you think are committed to voting for the Democratic candidate what their plan is for voting. Isn't it as simple as voting on Election Day? Nope.

EARLY VOTING

Most states now allow you to vote early, before Election Day. A quick Google search will tell you the rules in your state. Early voting could be by mail, where you request a ballot you fill out at home and mail back to election officials. Or it could mean going to an early voting site and casting a ballot there in the weeks before the election. In many states, both options are available.

Encourage your friends and family to vote early if that is an option for them. Why? A bunch of good reasons. First, it gets the vote in the bank. Plenty of things can happen on

Election Day that might prevent people from voting. Someone could be laid up with the flu and can't get out of bed. Maybe someone has to work late and can't vote before the polls close. Maybe a child gets sick and there's no childcare, or a parent has a medical emergency. Whatever it is, it's life and things happen. Reduce the risk by encouraging people to vote early. Voting early also frees people to work as volunteers on Election Day if they are able. They can devote all their time to helping get the vote out, without having to take time off to go to their polling place and vote.

The more people who vote early, the fewer people our presidential campaign will have to be worried about on Election Day. Let's look at it at the precinct level. Say in a precinct in Florida, the campaign thinks it knows of 250 people who will definitely vote for our candidate. But because these are new voters, or people who have a history of voting sporadically, the campaign is concerned these people might not get out to vote. You might know people like this in your own family. They mean to vote, but they're not really in the habit and they forget, or they get busy, and it doesn't happen on Election Day. If 125 of those 250 end up voting early (and the campaign will spend a lot of time and energy getting them to do just that), then you have cut in half the number of people you need to focus on come Election Day. Which makes it easier to reach them, math being math.

The campaign will be mailing reminders to these target voters, sending out digital and social media ads, as well as running ads on television and radio meant to reach them. But most effective will be their own friends and family imploring them to cast a vote to defeat Trump.

Still, not everyone will have family members like you so committed to doing all they can to elect a new president. The next best thing will be volunteers reaching out to these voters and doing all they can to convince them to vote. Hopefully, you and the volunteers you've recruited will be part of that effort in the closing days and weeks of the campaign.

MAIN REASONS PEOPLE GIVE FOR NOT VOTING

PERCENTAGE OF VOTERS

25

TOO BUSY, CONFLICTING WORK OR SCHOOL SCHEDULE

20

15

NOT INTERESTED, FELT MY VOTE WOULD NOT MAKE A DIFFERENCE

10

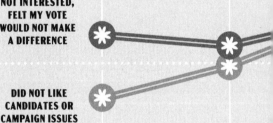

DID NOT LIKE CANDIDATES OR CAMPAIGN ISSUES

5

0

2000   2004

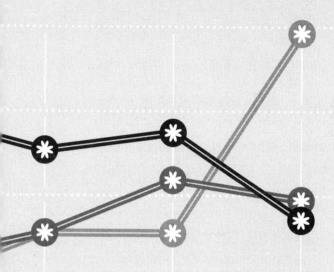

2008   2012   2016

GOTV IN BATTLEGROUND STATES

If you live in a battleground state or are volunteering in one or are helping to win battleground states from a distance, at the end of the campaign you'll most likely be working on GOTV efforts.

It will require lots of door knocking to reach these voters. And making phone calls. And sending personal postcards. We'll need to remind people when Election Day is and where their local polling place is. We'll let them know whether early voting is an option and how to do it. We'll find out whether they need a ride to the polls on Election Day and make sure they get one.

All of that is incredibly important. But the most valuable interaction may be when you talk to someone who says, "I don't like Trump, but what's the point? Nothing will change. I don't think I'm going to vote."

This is your chance. Tell the person why this election means so much to you.

Say that you understand the cynicism, but you believe our nominee can do good things and has the best interests of the country at heart. Maybe the person admits that they care about climate change or gun violence or health care. You can say for sure that a new president will make a difference in those areas. No matter what you say, the fact that *you* are saying it will make a difference.

When you as a young person are so passionate about the election, even though you can't vote in it, people will be inspired to get out there and vote, just as you've inspired people to register, to volunteer,

and to create and share content to support our candidate.

Maybe you even tell the reluctant voter to do it for you and kids like you, who need a chance at a better future.

On Election Day, when that person you talked to wrestles with whether to vote or not, they probably won't be thinking about the candidates, the debates, or the ads. They'll think of you. The young person who cared enough to knock on their door or call them. And that very well may be what gets them to walk or drive to their polling place and cast a vote they weren't sure they would cast.

No matter the result that night, you will still be responsible for strengthening our democracy and getting more people to exercise the sacred franchise of voting. And there is nothing more important than that.

9

ELECTION DAY

and

AFTER

THE FINAL HOURS

Depending on where you live, you might be in school on Election Day, or you might have the day off. Either way, there will be plenty to do. Polls will be open all day from the East Coast to the West. Sign up to do canvassing and phone calling in those final hours, either in battleground states or to help local Democratic candidates where you live. If you get a chance to do this, you might be surprised to find that you'll still reach people who don't know whether they are going to vote as the hours dwindle on the 2020 election. Treat your conversations with each of these citizens as if the fate of the republic depended on their decision. And in a very close election, it will. Tens of thousands of people like you, young and old, will be having similar conversations all over the country. Do all you can to convince these reluctant people that their vote matters, that it matters to you, that they can make the difference.

One of the **BEST** feelings in campaign work is to convince someone on Election Day to vote who **WASN'T GOING TO** or **WASN'T SURE.**

It's a good way to end a long campaign.

HOW TO SPEND ELECTION NIGHT

Once the work is done and the polls are closed, it's time to join most of America, and the world, in waiting for the results. It probably depends on where you live and how late you'll be able to stay up, but talk to your parents and other friends and family to decide how you want to witness it. Do you want to join other campaign volunteers and watch and wait for results where they are gathered? There will probably be a watching party hosted by the campaign in your area, which will hopefully turn into a victory party—does that sound like fun?

Maybe your family wants to host some close friends and family at your house. Or you'll go to a party someone else is hosting. Or maybe you want a quieter scene with just your parents and siblings. Whatever works for you is great, but have a plan!

It's an important night, and it will be a lifetime memory, win or lose.

Spend it in a way that will give you the most comfort and joy. And I'm certainly not beyond being superstitious when it comes to election night. Think about the place you can be—and the people you can be with—that will send the most good vibes and energy our nominee's way.

The one thing I would not suggest is staying in your room by yourself as the returns come in. Election nights have ups and downs. The numbers are confusing sometimes. You'll want to be around others to process what you are seeing, to get comfort when things are not looking good, and to share joy when they are. We all hope that at some point that night we'll find out America has elected a new president, our forty-sixth. You will want to hug, high-five, and laugh with others—you'll never forget those moments as long as you live.

In the worst-case scenario, where we come up short and Trump gets reelected, trust me, no one will want to go through that alone. We will need people to share our grief with, to cry and process with. We'll need to support each other and somehow find a way forward. Which we will, as hard and impossible as it may seem in the moment.

Election night is now often a multiscreen extravaganza. If you and your family are home or in a place where you have some control over the television, decide what network you want to watch as the results unfold. Research which news websites you want to refresh for detailed election results on the presidential race as well as local races. You might want to check social media feeds from election experts like Nate Silver and the team at FiveThirtyEight or the Upshot team at the *New York Times* as well as those from prominent journalists in your state who will be on top of all the results.

WHAT HAPPENS WHEN ELECTION NIGHT IS FINALLY OVER?

Working on campaigns is hard. Whether it's your job and it's all you do or whether you've just volunteered a few hours when you've had time. Everyone who has participated will be physically and mentally exhausted. You'll need a break. But not for long and certainly not for your lifetime.

DON'T STOP FIGHTING FOR WHAT YOU BELIEVE IN, EVER

Our country and the world will never reach its full potential and survive the climate change crisis unless enough young people get involved, stay involved, and fight for change. To be successful, new presidents always need the continuing support of everyone who helped them get to the Oval Office.

Keep posting on social media (or asking your family to post) when our new president does something you applaud or agree with; keep correcting the record when you see falsehoods (which will likely get more intense); keep reminding everyone you got to volunteer or vote that their time and effort was worth it by sharing when our next president follows through on a core promise.

Before you know it, we'll have the critical 2022 congressional elections coming up. Maybe a few readers of this book will have the opportunity to vote for the first time—so don't blow it! Make sure you do all the things you coached people to do in 2020.

Many of you may still be too young to vote in 2022, but get involved in those midterm elections. Find a local or state candidate you are passionate about and lend your time and talents as you did for this campaign.

Most important, in ways big and small, as you grow older and go through life, don't wait and don't assume you can't make a difference.

Run for office yourself. Manage a campaign. Become a journalist. Work at a nonprofit taking on voter protection and registration efforts.

Or simply be an engaged, insistent citizen.

Your generation has the chance to build on some of the progress my generation and others have made, but also to fix a lot of the problems we didn't tackle, or made worse. The entire world and generations to come will be rooting for you.

No generation before yours has ever been more intelligent, creative, worldly, or committed to protecting the planet and making it a place that everyone can live and thrive in, no matter what you look like, who you love, or where you come from.

YOU CAN DO THIS.

SOME HELPFUL RESOURCES

Websites

There are many sites here that will help you make sure your friends and family are registered to vote, find out how to register, and sometimes register right online. There are also sites that will help you find volunteer opportunities and ways to take action in your area.

Indivisible, INDIVISIBLE.ORG

I Will Vote, IWILLVOTE.COM

Mobilize America, MOBILIZEAMERICA.IO

Next Gen America, NEXTGENAMERICA.ORG

Rock the Vote, ROCKTHEVOTE.COM

Swing Left America, SWINGLEFT.ORG

Vote.gov, VOTE.GOV

Vote Save America, VOTESAVEAMERICA.COM

Books

Here are a few suggestions for books that focus on elections and voting if you want to learn more.

Goodman, Susan E. *See How They Run: Campaign Dreams, Election Schemes, and the Race to the White House*. New York: Bloomsbury USA, 2008.

Gutman, Dan. *The Kid Who Ran for President*. New York: Scholastic Paperbacks, 2012.

Roosevelt, Eleanor. *When You Grow Up to Vote: How Our Government Works for You*. New York: Roaring Brook Press, 2018.

Sobel, Syl. *Presidential Elections and Other Cool Facts*. Hauppauge, New York: B. E. S. Publishing, 2016.

Winter, Jonah. *Lillian's Right to Vote: A Celebration of the Voting Rights Act of 1965*. New York: Schwartz & Wade, an imprint of Random House Children's Books, 2015.

Infographic Credits

pp. 36–37: public domain; pp. 80–81: Brennan Center for Justice; pp. 88–89: Pew Voter Frequency Survey, The Pew Charitable Trusts; pp. 126–127: International Federation of Library Associations and Institutions, Factcheck.org; pp. 150–151: U.S. Elections Project; pp. 154–155: Pew Research Center; pp. 160–161: Pew Research Center.

ACKNOWLEDGMENTS

First, I want to thank my family. When I raised the idea of writing not one but two books through the better part of 2019, Olivia, Everett, and Vivian not only assented but did so enthusiastically. Election Night 2016 was one of the lowest moments our family has shared. If even a few words could make a difference in the next election, they were all in.

Olivia gave valuable feedback and advice after I was done with the first draft. I believe it's a much stronger book due to her keen insights. And more than anything, I wanted to write a book that Everett and Vivian would be proud of . . . or at the very least, not embarrassed by.

My agent at CAA, David Larabell, did not say I was crazy when I suggested that in addition to the adult book I was working on, *A Citizen's Guide to Defeating Donald Trump*, I work on a version for younger activists. He enthusiastically jumped right into it, helping shape the ultimate book and finding the right partner.

The folks at Macmillan have been that terrific partner. They took a leap of faith that I could craft something of interest and value to younger audiences. With their insights and expertise, I think we have.

Jean Feiwel and Laura Godwin have been steadfast supporters of this project from the get-go. Kate Farrell helped shape and improve the book immeasurably. Her enthusiasm for the project matched her talents and understanding of the audience. I hope all three of them take pride in the young activists who may be inspired to get more involved as a result of *Ripples of Hope*.

Lastly, I am inspired every day by young people, both in my home and around the world, who may be our last, best hope. I can't wait to see what you do.